The aim of the **Resources** is to enable students to develop their knowledge and understanding of the narrative structures of film and fictional television, and to be able to analyse texts using relevant narrative theories and key media terminology. The **Resources** will provide materials that outline key theories and ideas, and tasks and activities that encourage students to explore, discuss and analyse key texts. The choice of texts is by no means prescriptive, but the texts were chosen with the aim of providing a starting point or example for further study.

© Auteur 2006

Look at the following events (A):

I woke up at 7.30 on Friday morning.

It was pouring with rain.

The bus was crowded.

Now look at the following (B):

I woke up at 7.30 on Friday morning, half an hour later than usual.

It was pouring with rain so I decided to take the bus rather than walk.

The bus was crowded and late, so by the time I got to work I felt really stressed.

The difference between A and B is **causality**: three isolated events on their own do not make a story, but once we see them as a chain of events, each previous event directly affecting the next one, a story emerges.

The study of narrative involves studying the conventions and structures of stories represented in the media. We enjoy films and fictional television programmes because they tell stories. The patterns of events in films and television reflect the **chronology** and **causality** of events in our lives.

> * Chronology: the order of time.
> * Causality: the relationship between cause and effect.

Often we discuss the stories told in film and television with our friends and families. We tell each other what happened and why it happened.

TASK

In pairs, tell each other about a fictional television programme or film that you have watched recently.

* Did you remember everything that happened?
* Did you relate the events chronologically?

Most narratives are structured chronologically, often described as **linear** narrative. However you will study some texts that have non-linear narrative structures that make the ideas of causality and chronology less straightforward.

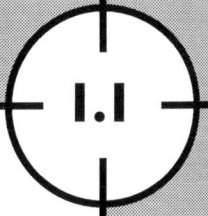

The Russian theorist, Victor Shklovsky, distinguished between the story and plot of a narrative. He used the following terms:

Fabula: Story – The chronological order of events.

Syuzhet: Plot – The structured events as they are presented to us.

The synopsis of a film that we read on a video or DVD cover, or in a film magazine, will tell us the plot of a film.

TASK

Write the plot of the last film you saw in the box. Use the arrows to add other information that might be included in the story.

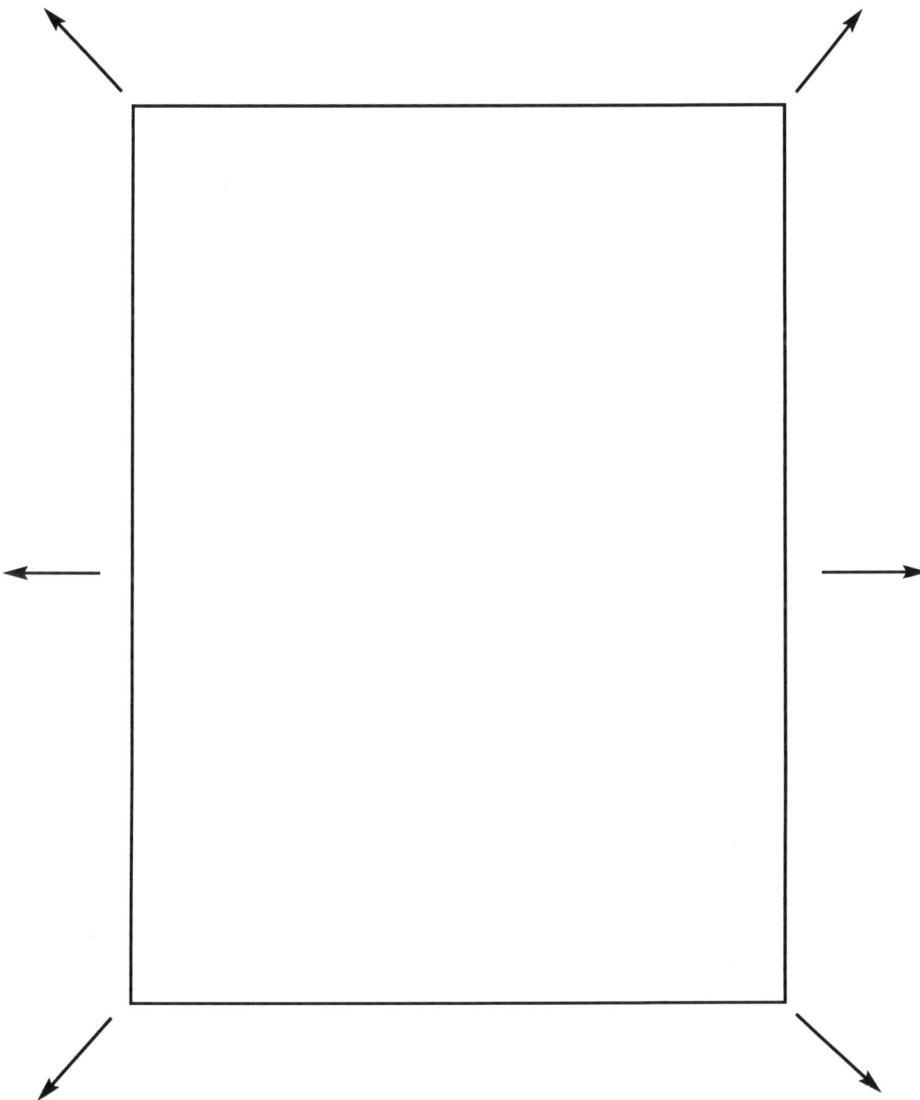

Introduction to narrative theories

Todorov's Structural Theory

Todorov believed that every narrative moves through a period of transformation in progressing towards its conclusion. A story begins with a particular state of affairs, then something happens to disrupt this state, and events finally close with a new state being reached. He broke this down into five distinct stages:

1. **Equilibrium or normality.**
2. **Disruption of the equilibrium.**
3. **Recognition of the disruption.**
4. **Attempts to repair the disruption.**
5. **Return to equilibrium/normality.**

The disruption of equilibrium motivates the cause/effect structure that comprises the plot of the film. Stages 2, 3 and 4 may be repeated many times over before we reach the final stage of equilibrium.

TASK

Think about the last film you saw. Can you identify the five stages of Todorov's theory?

1. Equilibrium:
2. Disruption:
3. Recognition of disruption:
4. Attempt to repair disruption:
5. Return to equilibrium:

Think about the following points:

- What effect does the disruption stage have on the audience?
- Who was responsible for the disruption?
- Who 'repaired' the disruption?
- How does the audience feel once the narrative has returned to equilibrium?

EXTENSION TASK

Most mainstream Hollywood films return to equilibrium. However, there are certain films that appear to return to equilibrium but then suprise us with either a sudden new disruption or leave us with the unsettling feeling that the return to equilibrium was not all it seemed. Consider the following films that follow this pattern: *Scream* (1996), *I Know What You Did Last Summer* (1997), *Alien* (1979).

- What do all these films have in common?
- Why do they follow this pattern?

TASK

Modern films that can be categorised by genre will usually follow this five stage structure. Based on your knowledge of film genres, write a brief description of typical events for each stage of the narrative for the following genres in the table below. The first box has been done for you.

	Equilibrium	Disruption	Recognition of disruption	Attempts to repair disruption	Return to equilibrium
Action	A busy city airport, everyone going about their daily lives.				
Horror					
Science fiction					
Romance					
Western					

Introduction to narrative theories

Propp's 'Structural' Theory

Vladimir Propp was a Russian critic and folklorist. He grouped characters and actions in narratives into seven character roles or 'spheres of action' and 31 functions that motivate the story.

Propp's character roles or 'spheres of action' are as follows:

Hero: Traditionally the male protagonist whose role it is to restore normality or equilibrium, defeating any villains and winning the love of the heroine.

Villain: The cause of the disruption and the antithesis of the hero, possibly also a threat to the safety and virtue of the heroine.

Dispatcher: This character sends the hero on his journey to restore equilibrium. The dispatcher may also be the father of the heroine, sending the hero on a quest to prove his worth before winning the heroine's love.

Donor: Gives the hero something to help him on his journey. This gift may be a piece of advice, a skill or an object such as a weapon.

Helper: Assists the hero in restoring equilibrium. The helper may be a sidekick, with the hero throughout, or someone he meets along the way.

Heroine: Usually a passive and vulnerable character, threatened by the villain and needing rescuing by the hero.

False hero: A character who initially seems to be on the side of the hero but who turns against him or deceives him.

Our experience of narratives from an early age leads us to be able to recognise these character roles. Not all of the character roles will be found in all narratives though and some narratives will feature updated versions of the more traditional roles.

TASK

Using your experience of narratives, think about the qualities that you would expect the following characters to have. Complete the following chart, outlining the main traits of each character.

	Qualities (e.g. brave)	Physical appearance	Typical clothes/colours
Hero			
Heroine			
Villain			

TASK

Watch the film *Pretty Woman* (1990), which has many of the characteristics of a modern fairy tale. Identify Propp's character roles within the film and make notes on how the characters fulfil their particular role. Write 500 words exploring how Propp's character roles can be applied to *Pretty Woman*.

Use the following chart to make notes as you watch the film:

Character in film	Propp's character role	Qualities of character	Physical attributes (including costume, setting, gestures)

EXTENSION TASK

Research the film biography of Julia Roberts.

- How typical is the character in *Pretty Woman* of Julia Roberts' film roles?
- What expectations do audiences have of a film that stars Julia Roberts?

EXTENSION TASK

Propp's character roles have their origins in folklore and fairy tales, and will need to be updated for modern narratives. For example, the role of the heroine has changed to reflect the changing representations of women. Watch a recent film that has a female protagonist, such as *Alien: Resurrection* (1997), *Speed* (1994) or *Kill Bill: Vol. 1* (2003) or *Kill Bill: Vol. 2* (2004). Write an analysis of how your chosen film has adapted its representation of the heroine role and also the other character roles as outlined by Propp.

Propp's 31 functions

	Function	Description
	Initial Situation	Members of family and/or hero introduced.
1	*Absentation*	One of the members of the family leaves home.
2	*Interdiction*	An interdiction (prohibition or decree) is addressed to the hero.
3	*Violation*	The interdiction is violated.
4	*Reconnaissance*	The villain makes an attempt at reconnaissance.
5	*Delivery*	The villain receives information about his victim.
6	*Trickery*	The villain attempts to deceive his victim.
7	*Complicity*	The villain submits to deception, unwittingly helping his enemy.
8	*Villainy*	The villain causes harm or injury to a member of the family.
	OR Lack	One member of the family lacks or wants something.
9	*Mediation*	The misfortune is made known and the hero is sent on his quest.
10	*Counteraction*	The hero agrees to counteraction.
11	*Departure*	The hero leaves home.
12	*1st function of donor*	The hero is tested.
13	*Hero's reaction*	The hero reacts to actions of future donor.
14	*Receipt of magical agent*	The hero acquires use of magical agent.
15	*Spatial transference*	The hero is led to object of search.
16	*Struggle*	The hero and villain join in direct combat.
17	*Branding*	The hero is branded (injured).
18	*Victory*	The villain is defeated.
19	*Liquidation*	Initial misfortune or lack is liquidated (brought to an end).
20	*Return*	The hero returns.
21	*Pursuit*	A chase: the hero is pursued.
22	*Rescue*	The hero is rescued.
23	*Unrecognised arrival*	The hero arrives unrecognised at home or in a strange place.
24	*Unfounded claims*	A false hero presents unfounded claims.
25	*Difficult task*	A difficult task is proposed to the hero.
26	*Solution*	The task is resolved.
27	*Recognition*	The hero is recognised.
28	*Exposure*	The false hero or villain is exposed.
29	*Transfiguration*	The hero is given a new appearance.
30	*Punishment*	The villain is punished.
31	*Wedding*	The hero is married and ascends the throne.

1.8

TASK

Watch a recent action film of your choice and identify Propp's 31 functions as they are represented in the narrative. (You may not find that every function is represented.) Consider how this structure helps your understanding of the narrative. Report back to your class on your findings.

Introduction to narrative theories

Claude Lévi-Strauss' Paradigmatic Structures

Propp's 31 functions and Todorov's five stages are examples of **syntagmatic** structures; they follow the order of events in a narrative.

Claude Lévi-Strauss argued that we should look below the surface of the text for the **paradigmatic** structures, the vertical structures within the text. He found that narratives are structured around conflict and oppositions, for example, hero versus villain. If we look at the themes and ideas associated with these character types, we can establish the following paradigmatic structures:

Hero	Villain
Good	Evil
Native	Outsider
Love	Hate
Handsome	Ugly

TASK

Complete the following paradigmatic structure for horror films:

Good	Evil
Day	
	Supernatural
Innocence	
	Black

Introduction to narrative theories

Barthes's Narrative Codes

Barthes outlined five codes that define the narrative. These codes act as clues for the audience, encouraging them to find answers and predict outcomes. The five codes are as follows:

Hermeneutic or enigma code: Narratives set up puzzles to be solved, e.g. 'What did the letter say?', 'Who killed the man?'. These enigmas or puzzles involve us in the narrative and help to create interest and anticipation. In most cases we will find out the answer to these enigmas and this will contribute to our enjoyment of the overall resolution.

Proairetic or action code: This code also relates to progression in the narrative and involves the codes of behaviour or actions that lead us to expect certain consequences, based on our experiences of other film narratives. For example, when a cowboy enters a saloon and takes his gun from its holster, this behaviour leads us to expect certain consequences, that someone will be shot.

Semic or semantic code: This code involves the connotative meaning of characters, objects or settings that we learn to 'read' through our experience of narratives. For example, the colour red is often used to suggest danger or passion; therefore, a red dress worn by a female character is likely to suggest her sexuality or power (Julia Roberts' character in **Pretty Woman** (1990)) and the red rose petals that cover the naked body of Angela Hayes (played by Mena Suvari) in **American Beauty** (1999) connote sexuality and sexual desire. In a similar way, we learn from experience that a handsome man in a film narrative will probably be the hero, and that a disfigured character is likely to be evil. Iconographic features of a text work in the same way, as we read objects and make links with genre, for example, a space ship will suggest science fiction.

Symbolic code: This code relates to symbolic features of a text that signify oppositions and antitheses that exist in a narrative (see Lévi-Strauss), such as good/evil, light/dark, civilised/savage. For example, in **Thelma & Louise** (1991), there is fundamental opposition between the male repressive world and the female escape; this is expressed symbolically through the interior, dark settings of male action and the exterior, light setting of Thelma and Louise's journey.

Cultural, or referential, code: This code refers to the world outside the text, and the knowledge that we commonly share and bring to the text to understand its meaning. For example, Baz Luhrmann's films **Moulin Rouge!** (2001) and **Romeo + Juliet** (1996) refer to a wide range of popular culture and historical events, as well as their actual historical/literary context and as audiences we use the cultural references to enhance our reading of the text. In a different way, many recent British films are set in the context of a particular historical event or era, such as **Billy Elliot** (2000), which is set against the background of the 1984 Miner's Strike, and **Brassed Off** (1996) and **The Full Monty** (1997), both of which deal with the decline in traditional British industries. Again, as audiences, our shared knowledge of these actual events informs our reading of the texts.

TASK

Barthes's Proairetic or Action Code

For each of the following actions, predict the likely outcome, based on your knowledge of film and television narratives:

Action	Outcome
A girl picks up a telephone and says 'Who is this?'	
A car screeches to a stop outside a building.	
A woman opens a letter and starts crying.	
A police officer runs to his car, strapping on his gun holster as he runs.	
A woman carefully applies lipstick in front of the mirror.	
The space station captain presses a series of buttons on the control panel.	
The sheriff throws the saddle on his horse and rides out of town.	
A young couple kiss passionately at a railway station.	

Classical Hollywood

The 'Golden Age' of Hollywood is generally considered to begin with the advent of sound in 1927 when The *Jazz Singer* was released. This era in Hollywood was dominated by the studio system, when major studios controlled production and distribution of films, and were also associated with particular stars and film genres. In 1948 a famous court case involving the major studio Paramount broke down this vertical integration, separating the studios from their production and distribution operations. This allowed independent film-makers and companies to start making more of an impact.

Key Terms

Vertical Integration: when one media company (e.g. film production) owns another media company involved in a different area of the media (e.g. film distribution), allowing them to dominate the market. A modern example is Time Warner.

Horizontal Integration: when a company takes over its competitors in the same industry, for example a major film studio taking over a smaller studio.

The methods of film-making during the 'Golden Age' of Hollywood established the narrative style that has become known as the 'Classical' Hollywood style. This style can be defined by the following points:

- Telling a story is the priority of a Classical Hollywood film.
- The story is told in an economic and seamless manner; that is, we will only be presented with necessary information.
- The narrative will focus on the cause/effect structure.
- The narrative will be motivated by an individual character's goals or desires.
- 'Real' time and space will be subordinated to the line of action; again, we will only be presented with necessary action.
- Events will be realistic in terms of the probability of events and record historical facts in a naturalistic way.
- Techniques of continuity editing are used to give the film its seamless narration. Key camera techniques such as the coverage process of shots (from establishing shot to extreme close-up), the 180 degree rule and the use of three point lighting were established during this period.
- The narrative will be unambiguous. All loose ends will be tied up and closure reached by the end; the goals or desires of the central character will be achieved.
- The ideology represented appeals to our fundamental belief in the triumph of the 'good guy'. The dominant ideology of the ideal of heterosexual love and marriage is also important.

Case Study: *Casablanca* (1942)

RESEARCH TASK

Casablanca was released in 1942. Using the internet or another source, find out some other titles of films released in this year. Identify common themes or genres and key stars.

Find some of the marketing images associated with *Casablanca*, for example, film posters, video and DVD cover images, etc. Make notes on your first impressions of narrative themes from these images.

Remind yourself of the following key points defining a Classical Hollywood film:

Telling a story is the priority of a Classical Hollywood film.

- The story is told in an economic and seamless manner; that is, we will only be presented with necessary information.
- The narrative will focus on the cause/effect structure.
- The narrative will be motivated by an individual character's goals or desires.
- 'Real' time and space will be subordinated to the line of action; again, we will only be presented with necessary action.
- The narrative will be unambiguous. All loose ends will be tied up and closure reached by the end; the goals or desires of the central character will be achieved.
- The ideology represented appeals to our fundamental belief in the triumph of the 'good guy'. The dominant ideology of the ideal of heterosexual love and marriage is also important.
- The above points all relate to the narrative structure and content.

TASK

Watch *Casablanca* and make detailed notes on how the above points are fulfilled in the film.

Remind yourself of the following point regarding the technical detail of a Classical Hollywood film:

- Techniques of continuity editing are used to give the film its seamless narration. Key camera techniques such as the coverage process of shots (from establishing shot to extreme close-up), the 180 degree rule and the use of three point lighting were established during this period.

Case Study: *Casablanca* (1942)

TASK

Watch the scene that begins straight after the Paris flashback up until Ilsa leaves Rick alone again. Using the storyboard layout on the following page, sketch each shot making notes on the technical detail. Photocopy the sheet as many times as necessary. You may need the following key words:

High-key Lighting	**Extreme Close-up (ECU)**	**Tracking Shot**
Low-key Lighting	**Big Close-up (BCU)**	**Zoom (In or Out)**
Key Light	**Close-up (CU)**	**Tilt**
Fill Light	**Medium Close-up (MCU)**	**Pan**
Back Light	**Medium Shot (MS)**	**Shot/Reverse Shot**
	Medium Long Shot (MLS)	**Cut**
	Long Shot (LS)	**Jump Cut**
	Very Long Shot (VLS)	**Cutaway**
	Two Shot	
	Over the Shoulder Shot	
	High Angle Shot	
	Low Angle Shot	

Shot	Shot	Shot
Description	Description	Description
Shot	Shot	Shot
Description	Description	Description

2.4

Case Study: *Casablanca* (1942)

TASK

Using all the information you have gathered on **Casablanca**, write 1000 words exploring how the film fulfils our expectations of a Classical Hollywood film.

Modern Hollywood, whose mainstream output dominates our cinema and rental viewing, operates largely along generic criteria as opposed to a studio system. While certain studios are still known for certain types of film (e.g. Disney), there is no longer a strict alignment between genre and studio. However, this genre-based film production can be seen as systematic in its own way as many genres have become so formulaic and predictable. There are exceptions of course, and many genres have merged or work together to form hybrids. In terms of narrative though, certain structures are established once a film is labelled by genre, which lead audiences to have certain expectations regarding plot events and outcomes.

Applying Todorov to Modern Hollywood Films

Todorov's 'five stage' theory:

1. **Equilibrium or normality.**
2. **Disruption of the equilibrium by a significant event.**
3. **Recognition of the disruption.**
4. **Attempts to repair the disruption.**
5. **Return to equilibrium/normality.**

Todorov's 'five stage' theory can be applied to almost any mainstream Hollywood film, but with some variation and repetition of the middle three stages.

TASK

Remind yourself of Torodov's five stages. In pairs, consider the following questions based on your knowledge of modern Hollywood films:

- What is the typical disruption (event) in a science fiction film, a horror film and an action film?
- Who is usually responsible for the disruption (which character role)?
- Who usually repairs the disruption?
- What effect does the repeat of the disruption/attempt to repair sequence have on the audience watching the film?
- What is the usual experience for the audience at the end of a Hollywood film?
- Why do we continue to watch and enjoy Hollywood films that have such predictable structures?

Three popular genres are romance, action and horror. The following outlines show the typical narrative structures of these genres according to Todorov's five stages:

Romance

Equilibrium: State of incompleteness/loss/lack for protagonists.

Disruption: Lack/loss made unsustainable/protagonists meet and clash.

Realisation of disruption: Protagonists obviously drawn to one another but resist and distract themselves through own attempts to repair loss/lack.

Attempts to repair disruption: Friends/protagonists themselves seek to repair lack/loss while man/woman continue to clash, but less and less resolutely (i.e. they are meant to be).

Return to (new) equilibrium: They fall in love, kiss, get married.

Action

Equilibrium: Public urban specific place, e.g. an airport, with everyone going about daily lives.

Disruption: The villain (an outsider/subversive) seeks to destroy the place through violence.

Realisation of disruption: The hero (usually uniformed) is called in/happens to be there and immediately begins quest to get the villain.

Attempts to repair disruption: Frequent clashes between hero and villain, repeated to maintain anticipation of 'will he/won't he' save the day.

Return to equilibrium: Peace is restored and the public are reunited with their daily routine.

Horror

Equilibrium: Often only an establishing shot of normality/the setting (e.g. *I Know What You Did Last Summer* (1997) – the establishing shot of the cliff by the sea is then followed by a zoom into a mysterious figure which signals disruption).

Disruption: Immediate fright/attack leading to immediate tension, followed by apparent equilibrium which is actually very shaky and unstable.

Realisation of disruption: Quite gradual – suspicions aroused, central characters might set out to 'solve' the mystery (especially in the popular hybrid of teen horror).

Attempts to repair disruption: The threat becomes more tangible and a definite sense of 'protagonists versus evil' develops.

Return to equilibrium: Return to state of safety, evil apparently vanquished …or is it? (Many horror films form part of a series so the return to equilibrium is not always complete, preparing us for the sequel.)

Case Study: *When Harry Met Sally (1989)*

When Harry Met Sally is a romantic comedy. The categorising of this film as romance leads us to have particular expectations regarding the narrative structure and content. With a typical Hollywood romance we would expect the following outline:

1. Equilibrium: State of incompleteness/loss/lack for protagonists.

2. Disruption: Lack/loss made unsustainable/protagonists meet and clash.

3. Recognition of disruption: Protagonists obviously drawn to one another but resist and distract themselves through own attempts to repair loss/lack.

4. Attempts to repair disruption: Friends/protagonists themselves seek to repair lack/loss while man/woman continue to clash, but less and less resolutely (i.e. they are meant to be).

5. Return to (new) equilibrium: They fall in love, kiss, get married.

Stages 2, 3 and 4 may be repeated a number of times to create anticipation for the audience, that sense of 'will they/won't they' fall in love.

These five stages can be applied to *When Harry Met Sally*, but you will find that the narrative is complicated by the time-span of the narrative, the fact that the plot covers 11 years and is divided into six episodes of time.

TASK

Detailed Analysis of *When Harry Met Sally*

You will need to watch the film more than once to carry out your detailed analysis.

Watch *When Harry Met Sally* and identify the five narrative stages according to Todorov's theory. Note when each stage starts and be aware of plot details that signify each stage (including dialogue, setting, actions, mise-en-scène).

Go back to the film, this time paying attention to the documentary-style interviews that are used to signify the start of each episode of time. Consider the following:

*   How do the episodes of time fit in with the five narrative stages?
*   What effect do the documentary-style interviews have on our response to the narrative?

Consider the following narrative devices and think about how they add to our understanding of the film.

*   Compare the false resolution (the first New Year's Eve) with the final resolution (the second New Year's Eve). What has changed?
*   *When Harry Met Sally* uses montage, split screen and voiceover. Find examples of these techniques in the film and think about their effect on the narrative.

Case Study: *When Harry Met Sally* (1989)

Soundtrack

There are two types of musical score found in fictional films: first, and more traditionally, there is the score composed specifically for the film; and second, there is the soundtrack of pre-existing music chosen by the film-maker. **When Harry Met Sally** has a soundtrack that consists of pre-existing music. The music in **When Harry Met Sally** is jazz standards, mainly performed by Harry Connick, Jr.

Jerrold Levinson in his essay 'Film Music and Narrative Agency' outlined two key issues that we should consider when thinking about film soundtracks:

> With appropriated scores the issue of specific imported associations, deriving from the original context of composition or performance or distribution, rather than general associations carried by musical style or conventions, is likely to arise.

> With appropriated as opposed to composed scores, there will, ironically, generally be more attention drawn to the music, both because it is often recognised as appropriated and located by the viewer in cultural space, and because the impression it gives of chosenness, on the part of the film-maker, is greater.

The second point relates to **When Harry Met Sally**: we are more aware of the soundtrack because it contains songs that we recognise and the songs chosen conjure up a particular mood for us.

Consider the following points:

*   What atmosphere is conjured up by the particular use of jazz classics in **When Harry Met Sally** (as opposed to any other music genre)? How does this influence the effect of the narrative on an audience?
*   How important are the lyrics of the songs used in **When Harry Met Sally**?

Further Comparative Work

Listen to an instrumental soundtrack for a film that you have not seen, perhaps **The Piano** (1993). As you listen, brainstorm any ideas that the soundtrack provokes in terms of mood, atmosphere and narrative structures. Then watch the film and consider the actual effect of the soundtrack on the narrative.

TASK

Use the above analysis to write a response of between 800 – 1000 words on how **When Harry Met Sally** fulfils our expectations of a romantic comedy in terms of its narrative structures.

Case Study: *Star Wars* (1977)

Star Wars is a science fiction film. It has a linear narrative structure and is focused around one of the most fundamental story types, that of a quest or journey.

An analysis based on Todorov's five stages would lead us to expect the following from a science fiction film:

1. **Normality or equilibrium:** A state of calm or well-being; this can be in our world or any other imagined world.

2. **Disruption:** A threat or meeting or appearance from an outside or 'alien' being; the word 'alien' is used loosely here as the agent of disruption will depend on the particular film.

3. **Recognition of disruption:** This is often a scientific or intellectual response, but with subsequent physical back-up.

4. **Attempts to repair disruption:** Physical conflict – the need to destroy the agent of disruption.

5. **Return to normality/equilibrium:** The world/society is restored to calm and safety.

TASK

Think of a science fiction film you have seen recently and consider how it fulfils our expectations of narrative structure.

Case Study: *Star Wars* (1977)

Propp's Character Roles

Hero: Traditionally the male protagonist whose role it is to restore normality or equilibrium, defeating any villains and winning the love of the heroine.

Villain: The cause of the disruption and the antithesis of the hero, possibly also a threat to the safety and virtue of the heroine.

Dispatcher: This character sends the hero on his journey to restore equilibrium. The dispatcher may also be the father of the heroine, sending the hero on a quest to prove his worth before winning the heroine's love.

Donor: Gives the hero something to help him on his journey. This gift may be a piece of advice, a skill or an object such as a weapon.

Helper: Assists the hero in restoring equilibrium. The helper may be a sidekick, with the hero throughout, or someone he meets along the way.

Heroine: Usually a passive and vulnerable character, threatened by the villain and needing rescuing by the hero.

False hero: A character who initially seems to be on the side of the hero but who turns against him or deceives him.

Star Wars has a quest narrative and has many similarities to myths and legends in its characters and story content. It is therefore appropriate to apply the theories of Vladimir Propp to this text.

Case Study: *Star Wars* (1977)

TASK

Watch *Star Wars* and use the following table to identify the character roles as they appear in the film.

Character role	Character in *Star Wars*	How do they fulfil this character role?
Hero		
Heroine		
Villain		
Dispatcher		
Donor		
Helper		
False hero		

3.7

Case Study: *Star Wars* (1977)

As you watch *Star Wars*, identify Propp's 31 Functions as and when they are fulfilled by the narrative. You may not find that all of them are in evidence, but you should find that they appear in chronological order.

	Function	
	Initial situation	
1	Absentation	
2	Interdiction	
3	Violation	
4	Reconnaissance	
5	Delivery	
6	Trickery	
7	Complicity	
8	Villainy OR Lack	
9	Mediation	
10	Counteraction	
11	Departure	
12	1st function of donor	
13	Hero's reaction	
14	Receipt of magical agent	
15	Spatial transference	
16	Struggle	
17	Branding	
18	Victory	
19	Liquidation	
20	Return	
21	Pursuit	
22	Rescue	
23	Unrecognised arrival	

24	Unfounded claims	
25	Difficult task	
26	Solution	
27	Recognition	
28	Exposure	
29	Transfiguration	
30	Punishment	
31	Wedding	

TASK

Write a detailed analysis of *Star Wars*, discussing how Propp's theories influence our understanding of the narrative.

Postmodern Narratives

Cinema audiences have certain expectations when it comes to narrative structure; we expect a chronological story to be told in a linear sequence of plot events leading to a logical and resolved conclusion.

Films that are labelled as postmodern play with our expectations of narrative structure, cinematic conventions and character types. The following list outlines some of the features of postmodern films:

- Non-linear or fractured narrative structures.
- Intertextuality with other media forms, for example, animation.
- Lack of resolution.
- Lack of time or space context.
- Lack of recognisable character types.
- Obvious editing or other technical detail.

Pulp Fiction (1994) is a film that can be labelled postmodern because it defies these expectations by playing around with our expectations of causality and time, presenting us with a fractured narrative whose logic only becomes clear in retrospect.

The Russian theorist, Victor Shklovsky, distinguished between the story and plot of a narrative. He used the following terms:

Fabula: Story – The chronological order of events.

Syuzhet: Plot – The structured events as they are presented to us.

Case Study: *Pulp Fiction* (1994)

Pulp Fiction involves three interlocking stories. The narrative of the film is structured into the following five parts:

1. Prologue.
2. Vincent Vega and Marcellus Wallace's Wife.
3. The Gold Watch.
4. The Bonnie Situation.
5. Epilogue.

These parts do not follow the chronological story, which can be disorientating for audiences used to linear narratives. *Pulp Fiction* makes us more conscious of the difference between plot and story than other films.

TASK

Watch *Pulp Fiction* and then discuss your initial reactions to the film in terms of content, characters and narrative structure.

TASK

This sheet outlines the plot in the order it is presented to us. Cut this sheet into strips and re-order according to the chronological story structure.

Consider the following questions:

- How does the chronological story structure change our response to the narrative?
- Why do you think Tarantino chose not to follow a linear structure?
- Can we apply Propp's character functions to *Pulp Fiction*?
- What is our response as an audience to the characters in *Pulp Fiction*?

Honey Bunny and Pumpkin are eating breakfast in a typical American diner. They decide to rob the diner.

✂..

Jules and Vince go to Brett's apartment to pick up the briefcase and kill Brett.

✂..

Marcellus Wallace pays Butch to fix the boxing match. Jules and Vince arrive dressed in shorts and T-shirts.

✂..

Vince's date with Mia Wallace.

✂..

Captain Koons visits the young Butch to present him with his father's gold watch.

✂..

The boxing match. Butch returns to Fabienne, but in the morning discovers that she did not bring his gold watch. He goes back to his apartment to get it, discovers Vince and kills him.

✂..

Butch and Marcellus Wallace being tortured in the Mason Dixon Pawnshop.

✂..

Butch leaves the city with Fabienne on Zed's chopper.

✂..

Brett's apartment. The fourth man emerges from the bathroom after Brett is killed, shoots at Vince and Jules, but then is killed by them. Jules experiences 'divine intervention'.

✂..

Marvin is shot in the back of the car.

✂..

Mr Wolf helps Jules and Vince clean up the car at Jimmy's house.

✂..

Jules and Vince go to the diner for breakfast. They intervene in Honey Bunny and Pumpkin's robbery.

✂..

Jules and Vince leave the diner.

✂..

4.2

Case Study: *Run Lola Run* (1999)

Watch **Run Lola Run** (1999), written and directed by Tom Twyker. Lola's boyfriend Manni is in big trouble. He works for a big-time gangster and has bungled a big deal by leaving 100,000 DM on the subway. Lola has 20 minutes to save Manni from his fate. In the film, Lola's 20 minute dash to save Manni is replayed three times, offering three possible outcomes. As you watch the film, make detailed notes on the contrast between the representation of the following events:

- Lola running out of her apartment.
- Lola going to the bank to ask her father for money.
- Lola reaching Manni.

For each event, compare the action, technical detail, sound and audience response in a table like the one below:

	Action	Technical detail (for example,	Sound and soundtrack	Audience response
Lola running out of the apartment				
Lola going to the bank to ask her father for money				
Lola reaching Manni				

Case Study: *Run Lola Run* (1999)

EXTENSION TASK

Think about the following to write a detailed analysis of **Run Lola Run**:

- What overall effect do the contrasting outcomes have on the audience response to the film?
- What point (if any) do you think that the film is trying to make?
- How does Run Lola Run fulfil our expectations of a postmodern film?

Use the following qualities of a postmodern film as a guideline:

- Non-linear or fractured narrative structures.
- Intertextuality with other media forms, for example, animation.
- Lack of resolution.
- Lack of time or space context.
- Lack of recognisable character types.
- Obvious editing or other technical detail.

4.4

Postmodern Text and Institution

Pulp Fiction and *Run Lola Run* can both be seen as postmodern films. They both have unconventional narrative structures and subvert technical conventions, creating a disorientating and distancing effect for audiences.

Mainstream Hollywood genre films are produced and distributed by the major Hollywood studios and intended for mass audiences. Films that can be labelled post-modern or independent are likely to be produced by small or independent production companies.

The following outline shows the institutional context for each film:

	Production Company	**Distribution Company**
Pulp Fiction	A Band Apart	Miramax Films
	Jersey Films	Buena Vista International
	Miramax Films	
Run Lola Run	X-Filme Creative Pool	Bavaria Film International
	Westdeutscher Rundfunk (WDR)	Columbia TriStar
	arte	Sony Pictures Classics

Think about the following:

- Find out the status of the companies involved in the two films.
- Despite being produced by small production companies, both films (particularly *Pulp Fiction*) have managed to reach international audiences and achieve critical and financial success. How have they managed this?
- Research the production and distribution companies involved in two mainstream Hollywood films. How do they compare to the companies involved in *Pulp Fiction* and *Run Lola Run*?
- Why do you think that unconventional films are less likely to be produced by the major studios?

TASK

Comparative Study

Identify a postmodern film, a Classical Hollywood film and a modern Hollywood genre film. Watch your chosen films and make detailed notes based on the headings in the chart on the following page.

Write a detailed comparative analysis of your three films, discussing the different narrative structures and their effect on audiences.

	Classical Hollywood	Modern Hollywood	Postmodern
Narrative structure			
Character types			
Editing			
Soundtrack			
Resolution			
Ideology			
Institutional context			

5.0

The key differences between film narratives and fictional television narratives are as follows:

Film	Television
A complete story, with the expectation of resolution at the end (so-called 'closed' narrative). Audiences watch a film in one sitting.	Multiple stories, which may or may not be resolved within one episode (so-called 'open' narrative). Audiences retain information and wait for resolution.
A few core characters, with other minor characters. Audience expect certain types of character as defined by Propp. This makes them instantly recognisable and avoids the need for lengthy development.	Many characters, with information fed gradually over time. Characters will be more 'real' in the sense that they will change behaviour as stories develop, rather than adhering to a particular role. However, stereotypes do exist in some television narratives, e.g. soap operas, which aid easy recognition and enable audiences to form allegiances.
Time is not naturalistic: events may take place over a day, weeks or years. Audiences suspend existence in real time to accept the time sphere of the film text. As such, events can also be unrelated to real life, but have generic verisimilitude	Time is often naturalistic, for example, soap operas will often follow the days of the week and seasons and key real events, e.g. Christmas, will be referred to. Story events will be more likely to reflect plausible 'real life' events.

Fictional Television Narratives – The Soap Opera

Key features of soap opera narratives:

- They are potentially never ending: a soap opera is set in a permanent location which allows characters and events to interplay in endless possible narratives.
- Soap operas focus on communities rather than individuals, although narratives will focus on individual characters within the community.
- Soap operas follow the lives of many characters so there will be many narratives going on at once.
- Short-term events may be resolved within a single episode, others will continue over many days, weeks or months.
- The typical equilibrium/disequilibrium/equilibrium structure may not be contained within a single episode; this means that audience interest is maintained between episodes.
- Narrative tension is often built up towards the end of a week's episodes to maintain interest over the weekend.

TASK

Identify all the soap operas currently running on terrestrial channels. As a class, discuss the following:

1. Identify the location for each soap opera.
2. Discuss the type of community represented in each soap opera. You may refer to issues such as age, class, ethnic group.
3. Identify some characters from each soap opera. Discuss character types that are common in soap opera.
4. Identify the scheduling for each soap opera and make suggestions for the target audience of each soap opera.

5.2

Fictional Television Narratives – The Soap Opera

TASK

Watch all the episodes in one week of a soap opera of your choice. Chart the narratives that are current in that particular week.

- How many narratives were involved in this week?
- Which narratives were resolved?
- What kind of narratives are continuing?
- Did narrative tension build as the week progressed?

Analysing Narratives in Soap Opera

Chosen soap opera...

Dates of analysis...

Day	Narrative strands	Active or resolved?

Case Study: Soap Opera Simulation

To develop your knowledge and understanding of the narrative structures that exist in soap operas, you are going to devise your own soap opera and write a treatment for the first week's episodes of that soap opera. Work through the Case Study, completing each task.

TASK 1

Research three soap operas of your choice. For each soap opera watch at least one episode. Complete the following table:

Soap opera	Location	Typical characters	Typical storylines

Consider the following statements:

- Most soap operas focus on a small community, either in a city (*Eastenders*, *Coronation Street*, *Brookside*, *Neighbours*) or a village (*Emmerdale*).

- British soap operas tend to focus on working class characters, whereas American and Australian soap operas feature middle class and often wealthy characters.

- The storylines will depend on the location, e.g. *Emmerdale* will feature storylines that are relevant to the rural community, while storylines in *Eastenders* will reflect city life.

- Soap characters are often constructed based on stereotypes: the 'jack-the-lad' young man, the moaning old woman, the single mother, the stroppy teenager.

- Soap operas reflect the realistic living status of audiences: not everyone lives in nuclear families and you will find examples of shared households, extended families and lone parent families.

Think about your research of three soap operas. What evidence did you find of the points made in the statements above?

TASK 2

Having completed the research task and studied three soap operas in detail, you are ready to start devising your own soap opera.

You need to decide on the following:

1. Location

_____

2. Five households (try to vary the types of people within each household):

_____

_____

_____

_____

_____

_____

3. Storylines for a week's schedule. Think carefully about the narrative structures of the soap operas you have studied so far. Consider the variety of resolved and ongoing narratives that might exist within a single episode. You may wish to plan this task on paper before completing the following chart:

Episode	Narrative strands	Active or resolved?

TASK 3

Evaluate your soap opera, discussing how it uses the conventions of soap operas in terms of narrative structures and character types. Refer to at least two other soap operas and compare your ideas with your chosen soap operas.

5.6

Fictional Television Narratives – The Series

Key features of a series are as follows:

- The narrative of a series is cyclical; it will reach a resolution at the end of each episode.

- The episode will have a theme or title that is the focus for that particular episode.

- Series are set in a permanent place such as a police station or hospital.

- Series have a mixture of permanent and temporary characters; narratives involving the permanent characters will run over between episodes, whereas narratives involving temporary characters will be specific to one episode.

TASK

Look at a television guide for a week. Identify all the series on the four main terrestrial channels (BBC 1, BBC 2, ITV, Channel 4) for that week. Group them into genres (e.g. crime, medical).

Watch one episode of a series from your chosen week. Evaluate the series in terms of the key features outlined above. Make notes in the chart on page 5.7.

Fictional Television Narratives – The Series

Series..

Location	
Permanent characters	
Main temporary characters in chosen episode	
Storylines involving permanent characters	
Storylines involving temporary characters	
Theme of episode	
Channel and schedule slot	
Target audience	

5.8

Case Study: Television Series

Television series may have many similar features and conventions in terms of their narrative structures, but may differ greatly in terms of their style and production, depending on the broadcasting institution and target audience. For this Case Study you are going to carry out a detailed analysis of two series of your choice; the series will be the same genre but produced by different institutions for different audiences. Suggested comparisons might be **_Casualty/ER_**, **_The Bill/NYPD Blue_**.

Your teacher will give you two copies of the following chart for you to make notes under relevant headings. You are only required to watch one episode of each series, but you may wish to watch your chosen episode more than once.

TASK

Write a detailed response to the following question:
Compare two television series. Explore the differences in narrative structures and techniques and evaluate how these have been influenced by the institutional context. Identify the target audience for each text and discuss the appeal of each text for its target audience

Series title ....

Episode title and date ....

Synopsis		
Narrative structure	**Camera**	
	Sound	
	Mise-en-scène	
	Editing	
Institution		
Actors		
Production values		

The 'One-off' or Single Drama

The following chart outlines the key differences between film and television single dramas in terms of narrative structures and effect on audience:

Film	One-off or single drama on television
Represents an escape into an unreal world, where emotions are heightened and audience responses are more aspirational.	More realistic, closer to home, audiences more likely to identify with characters and events.
Identified by genre, leading to expectations regarding plot, setting, character and narrative structure.	More likely to be plot or character-driven, often with a political or social edge, which prevents it being typecast.
Faster, action-driven pace, special effects, quick progression through equilibrium/disequilibrium structure.	Slower moving, relying on audience interest in characters and their motivation. Belief in the greater realism of characters.
Higher budget, more access to special effects, stars, expensive sets and locations. Heightens aesthetic experience for audience but distracts from close attention to narrative.	Lower budget, therefore restricted in terms of stars and effects, but greater realism and physical actuality in terms of location.
Tend to be watched with peers as a social occasion, which influences level of involvement with the narrative.	A more serious viewing experience, possibly alone, so the depth of emotional response is heightened by uninterrupted attention given.
Tend to follow Todorov's five stage structure, ending in a satisfying resolution, emphasising the 'feel-good' factor of film viewing.	More disruptive and disturbing in terms of narrative structure, not necessarily reaching a positive conclusion.

5.10

The 'One-off' or Single Drama

Watch a recent television single drama that was shown on one of the four main terrestrial channels. Make brief notes under the following headings, identifying its key features and conventions:

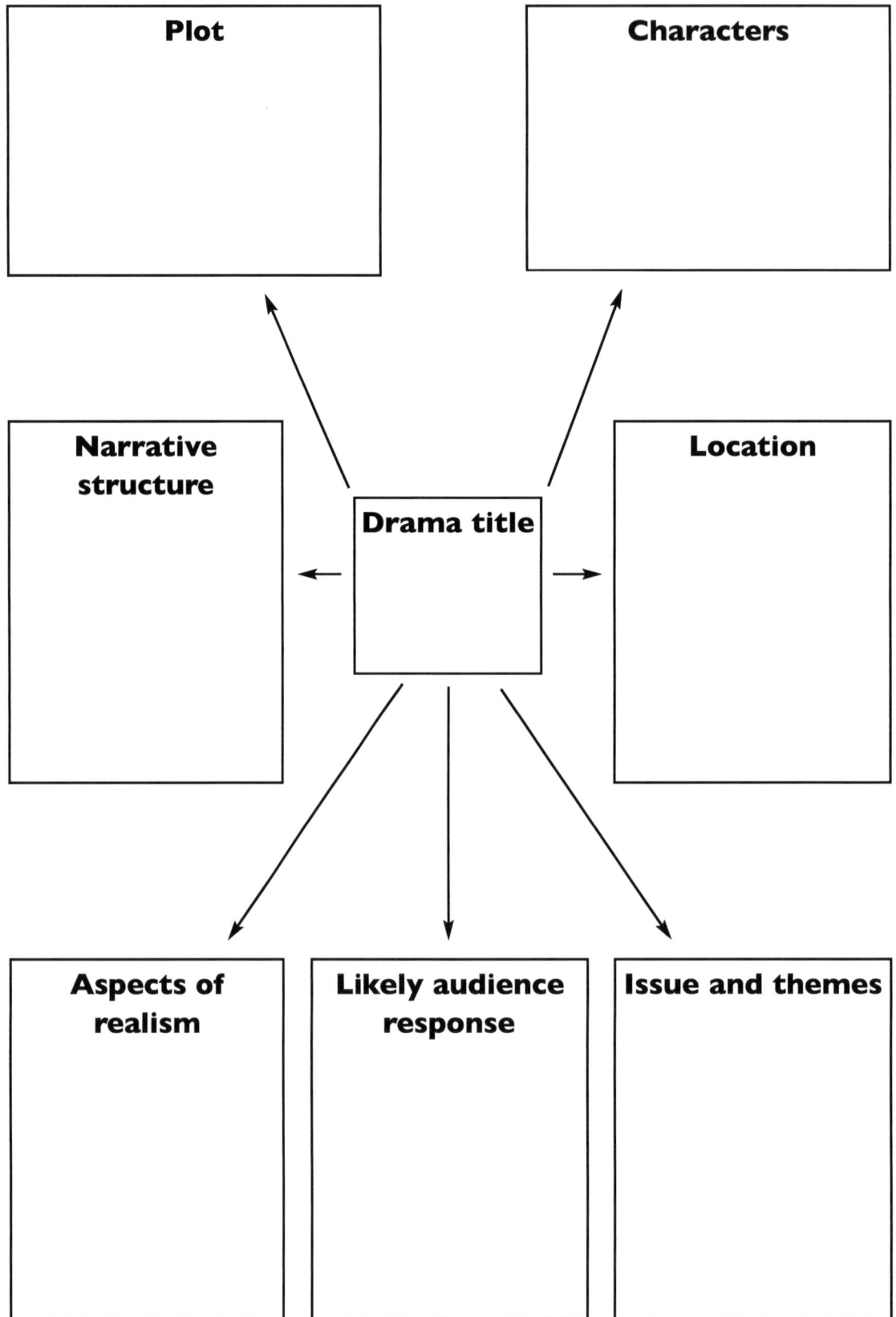

Plot

Characters

Narrative structure

Drama title

Location

Aspects of realism

Likely audience response

Issue and themes

6.0

Technical Conventions of Fictional Television

Although fictional television includes many different genres, there are certain technical conventions that mainstream audiences expect in their experience of the narrative. These include the following:

- A scenic structure.

- Objective positioning of the camera: we expect to watch the narrative from an observational position, i.e. we do not expect any character to address us directly.

- No 'dead' time: fictional television, due to the constraints of scheduling and the time-slots allocated for each text, does not tend to mirror real time. Scenes will involve key events and dialogue, rather than incidental or inconsequential action. Time will move on through the editing between shots, conventionally a straight cut.

TASK

However, there are also specific technical conventions found in the particular genres of fictional television that fulfil our expectations of the development of the narrative in those genres. Select a current programme from each of the main genres of fictional television and watch the opening 10 minutes, making detailed notes in the following table:

	Soap opera	Series	Serial	One-off drama
Camera				
Sound				
Editing				
Lighting				

TASK

Using the storyboard sheet, present the first minute of a fictional television text of your choice and write a detailed analysis of how the narrative is established and constructed.

6.1

Shot	Shot	Shot	Shot	Shot
Description	Description	Description	Description	Description
Shot	Shot	Shot	Shot	Shot
Description	Description	Description	Description	Description

Case Study: *The Office*

The Office is a fictional representation of an observational documentary, set in a paper company office in Slough. ***The Office*** relies on audiences experiences of different media forms and texts and is therefore an example of a text that uses **intertextuality**. It uses the technical structures of an **observational documentary**, combined with the narrative structure of a **series**. It is based on the recent popularity of docusoaps, where documentary techniques are used to follow the life of a real place such as an airport or a hospital.

The following techniques might be found in an observational documentary:

* Observational camera that appears to follow or eavesdrop on action.
* Straight-to-camera interviews where subjects have apparently been asked questions by an invisible documentary maker.
* Voice-over commentary.
* Focus on particular key workers creating a narrative of events.

TASK 1

Identify an observational documentary or docusoap on television. Watch an episode and make notes on any use of the techniques outlined above.

Think about the following:

* Why do audiences watch this text?
* What is the likely audience response to the text? For example, are we being encouraged to judge or empathise in a particular way?
* Does the text borrow any techniques from fictional television?

6.3

Case Study: *The Office*

TASK 2

Watch the first episode of the first series of ***The Office***.

Identify use of the following documentary techniques:

- Observational camera.
- Straight-to-camera-interviews.

Remind yourself of the following main qualities of a fictional television series:

- Workplace setting.
- Core group of permanent characters.
- Episodic structure with cyclical narrative structure within each episode.
- Ongoing storylines involving permanent characters.

Create a brainstorm of how ***The Office*** uses both documentary techniques and qualities of fictional television series.

The narratives established in the first episode of ***The Office*** fulfil our expectations of a television series because they set up problems (or disruptions) in the lives of the main characters that we presume will be resolved. In a table like the one below, outline the main narrative strands set up in the first episode and anticipate their likely progression and resolution:

Storyline	Characters involved	Likely development/outcome

Case Study: *The Office*

EXTENSION TASKS

The intertextuality of **The Office**, the non-fictional form of documentary, leads to a blurring of the boundary between reality and fiction. Consider the following possible aspects of realism within a text. How is realism constructed in **The Office**?

Verisimilitude: The verisimilitude of a text lies in its connection to reality in terms of what is real within our generic expectations (for example, science fiction allows us to accept certain technical dialogue as real) and our cultural expectations (for example, the text may reference real people or places).

Actuality: The actuality of the text lies in the sense of physical details, for example, setting, clothes, furniture, equipment.

Believability: This refers to the inner or emotional realism of characters and their motivation. The believability of characters enables audiences to identify with the situation portrayed.

Technical codes: We have learnt to accept certain technical codes and conventions as realistic for particular genres and media forms.

Consider the following:

*   What aspects of **The Office** make it appear to be 'real'?
*   What aspects of **The Office** make it appear to be fictional?

You may wish to watch other texts that use intertextuality in similar ways, mixing documentary techniques and style in a fictional format. Think about the narrative structures of the following texts and how the use of intertextuality affects the audience experience and response:

*   **The Truman Show**
*   **This Life**

Narrative and Institution

TASK

Look at a television guide covering the four main terrestrial UK channels, BBC1, BBC2, ITV and Channel 4. Find examples of fictional television within the week's schedule. Note down the relevant information in the following table:

	BBC1	BBC2	ITV	Channel 4
Soap opera				
Series				
Serial				
One-off drama				

Choose two channels for comparison and start to identify similarities and differences within their weekly schedules. You may wish to focus on: genre, target audience, time-slot, narrative content, narrative style, conventions.

Analyse your findings, thinking about how much institution affects the narrative of fictional television.

RESEARCH TASK

Look at the websites for a variety of television channels. Find out what their policies are for fictional programming. Identify programmes in their schedule that particularly support their policies.

Film Trailers

Analyse a variety of film trailers using the following discussion points:

- What is the institutional context for the film (i.e. production and distribution companies)?
- What is the genre of the film?
- What images from the narrative are represented in the trailer? What evidence of conflict/disruption is there?
- What enigmas are established for the audience?
- What oppositions are established for the audience?
- What examples of generic iconography do we see?
- What impression do we get of the audio-visual style of the film?
- What other techniques are used to establish and structure the narrative, for example, voice-over, on-screen graphics?
- Who are the target audience for the film?
- What is the USP of the film?

TASK

For a film that you have seen recently, storyboard an appropriate 30 second trailer for that film using the storyboard sheet. Analyse your own trailer using the bullet points above.

Audience Responses to Fictional Narratives

Write a media diary of your experiences of fictional media forms for a week. Record your experiences in the following table:

Text	Where I watched it	Why I watched it	Who with	Response

Audience Responses to Fictional Narratives (cont.)

The Uses and Gratifications model of audience response is based on the belief that audiences have certain needs that are fulfilled by the media. These are as follows:

- **Diversion:** Escape or release from every day life and concerns.
- **Personal relationships:** The media may be a focus for companionship, i.e. the event of listening to/watching something with another person; it may also form the basis for conversation.
- **Personal identity:** Identifying and comparing ourselves with characters, events and situations.
- **Surveillance:** Finding out information about the world.

TASK

Think about how many of the above 'needs' have been fulfilled by your engagement with fictional media texts in the week studied.

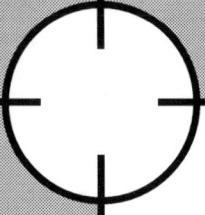